Fireflies

The Darkness of Grief and the Light That Remains

A Poetry Journal Exploring the Five Stages of Grief

Dr. Teruko Dobashi

When the paramedics pronounced my mother dead, they told us she had likely been gone for nearly forty-eight hours. At first, not hearing from her didn't seem unusual. My mother sometimes disappeared for days. Silence from her was not uncommon. But nothing prepares you for the moment when absence stops being temporary and becomes etched in permanent marker. Two nights before she died, I was performing at an open mic in Atlanta. That night, one of the poets read a piece about fireflies. He talked about catching them in jars as a child, about how they used to fill summer nights with small flashes of light and the joy he experienced. Then he said something that stayed with me. "Where have all the fireflies gone? Do they no longer believe we are worthy of their light?"

After the event, my partner and I talked about that particular poem during the drive home. We realized neither of us had seen fireflies in years. It felt strange, almost unsettling, like a small piece of childhood had quietly disappeared from the world.

Two days later, I received the call. My mother had overdosed. She was found in her car one block away from her apartment and less than two miles from the Tenderloin, where fentanyl plays Russian roulette with the souls of those who call San Francisco home. When the words settled in, my body collapsed beneath the weight of them. Gravity released me. Grief pinned me to the ground in a way I had never known before. Eventually I made it to the car, barely holding myself together. I sat in the passenger seat and screamed for my mother, begging for it all to be a lie. I just knew I would die from the weight of the pain alone.

And then something happened that I will never forget and probably half of you won't believe.

A firefly flew through the open passenger window. It landed on the steering wheel for a moment, glowing softly, before drifting back into the night.

For a brief second, the world held its breath. Time stood still. In that flicker of light, I felt a presence–a quiet reminder that my mother was still with me and always would be. Like she wanted me to know that she was fine, and I was going to be okay, too.

The Japanese word for firefly is Hotaru. In poetry, it often symbolizes passionate love and fleeting light in darkness. When I think about that kind of love, I think about my parents.

My father died fifteen months after my mother. Although, he spoke about how tired he was of dialysis and in general and looked weaker each time I visited him. I begged him not to leave me in the same year my mom passed, and somehow, he granted that wish. But deep down, I knew his heart had already begun its journey back to hers. My parents shared a love that burned brightly, the kind of love that leaves a permanent glow in the people who witness it.

This book is born from that light.
Grief moves through many stages: denial, anger, bargaining, depression, acceptance. But grief is not lineal. It does not follow a straight path. It flickers. It returns. It disappears and reappears when we least expect it.
Like fireflies in the dark.

This collection is my grief journal, but it is also an invitation. As you read, I hope you allow yourself to feel, to remember, and to write your own way through loss. No one can tell you how to grieve or when it will be over. But if you listen closely, you may find that the people we love never truly leave us. Their light continues to glow in the quiet places we carry inside. And sometimes, if we are lucky, it finds a way to appear right in front of us.

Like a firefly in the night.

This collection is dedicated to Regina Lynn Hamilton—

12/30/1962-07/21/2023

Mama,

You deserved a life better than the one you were given

I promise to keep your legacy alive

Not a day passes by

that I am not reminded

of the hustle and ambition

you planted and carefully cultivated in me

This light I carry

is yours.

Table of Contents

Denial

"Some have never been touched by the

light of a firefly"

Fine

If I don't say it out loud
grief will suffocate me
and tell others that I'm just fine

Not Dead

Not dead

just tired

carrying the weight of addiction

Heaviest when coming down

Falling forward

Not dead

just quiet

Phone on silent

We haven't heard from her in days

Not dead

just private

"Don't tell them people my business

Ima get clean—Lord be my witness"

Not dead

just crying

Tears-stained pillows

Still fresh

She just left home

Unmade bed

Lights still on

Lord, she can be missing

But please

Not dead—

The silence of the highway
The secrets of the streets
Where my workday and the interstate meet
your active listening is my retreat
My go to
My calm
The call to my mama
Triumph or defeat
We talk for hours
Here
all my worries take a backseat
Cruising in the HOV lane
Just you and me
Across state lines
If I didn't pick up
You'd call umpteen times
Now it's me
Blowing up your phone

Yesterday

The calendar has changed two times over
But it always feels like yesterday
When your name crosses
The tip of my tears
And sits in the center of my stories
I always speak of you in present tense

Optimism

I called you
Knowing you wouldn't answer
But optimism clutched my phone
Hoping to hear your voice once more
Grief left me longing for more
one more time to hear your voice
one more time to share my day
ask questions
Find myself lost in laughter
But here I am
Sitting on the edge of regret
Hanging on hope
Phone in hand
Denying anything
That feels too close to truth

The conversations don't have to stop. Write what you would share with your loved ones from today. Pause... imagine their response... talk to them often

Breathe

Grief is spontaneous

A smell

A song

A thought

One moment

you're laughing

And the next

You're

Clawing yourself out

from

Memories

trying

their best to suffocate you

I'll Call Tomorrow

Ripping and running
Running and ripping
The streets be her witness
Every time I plan to call
I remind myself she's just busy
Caught in the fast life
60 in the thirty
Pausing the truth
That I know
Will do me dirty
The reality that'll
Take me down under
Muddied and mortified
So, I'll keep reminding myself
To call her tomorrow

Message

Booty, mommy loves you to the moon
and back
You better pick up the phone
Teruko, you need to call me back
Remember to keep your head held
high
They gon hate anyway
so let them stare you in the eyes
You're beautiful— they just jealous
you better realize
Your dad and I made you from love
You're smart, but you better watch yo
mouth
I'm not one of your little friends
Talking like you den lost yo mind
You know I brought you in this world
And I'll take yo black ass out
Next breath...
You know you're my best friend
you can tell me anything
If they ever try to hurt you
I'll kill them dead

For you
I'd make my bed under the jail
Travel high to heaven and smoke with
the demons in hell
I'm telling you now
Don't start nothing but you better
finish it
Cause who hit harder
them or me?
It's almost my birthday
what you gonna get for me?
I want some boots, a Michael kors
purse, send me some cigarettes or a
few dollars
I know you not eating again
That's a damn shame
You know it's ok to miss a meal
I love you stank
Pick up the damn phone
Booty,
You better call me back

Before the Fall into Healing

I wonder if I never let the ground go

would it drain me of my hurt

Cover me in concrete comfort

Cloak the clock

so time stood still

I wonder how long it would take

For me to fall back into place

Stitch pieces of me

On the inseam of

Forgetfulness

Hardened

Wondering if I could still grow

I'm sitting on the edge of healing

Afraid to look down

Afraid "it'll get better" & that "I'll actually be ok"

"*Even fireflies burn when their light is trapped*"

Misplaced Hurt

Grief finds its reflection in razor blades

Tongue so sharp

But today...

I hope this pain chooses

to rip

Someone else apart

How have your words you've said to someone else during your time of grieving affected

someone you love? Do they deserve an apology? If so, tell them

Cold

Today grief swallowed me whole

Held me against its cheek

Crushed me under the weight of defeat

When I thought I'd never see light again

It spit me out

As if my tears were too salty

Body too numb

My wounds were too old

Stale

The world hardened me

Yet My Pain is still tender

But

Grief

like many

doesn't like its food too cold

Fireflies

Holidaze

Commercialism curates

Pain

pouring from ads

memories on sale

That I can no longer bargain for

Cards with cringeworthy words

Diamonds & drill sets

Holidays just won't let me forget

I feel you in the breeze

Hear you in the rumbling of the trees

Every song speaks to me

Reminds me of the freedom in your melody

Recently tears have caressed my face

More frequently

The wise and experienced

Said it would get better in time

These clocks must be standing still

Because I've gone through my first birthday,

Thanksgiving, and Christmas without you here

Not to mention

My first Mother's Day

Without you is near

I watch as the sun goes down

The calendar changes again

The leaves come back

Wishing you too

Were

My spring

Which holiday or season is the hardest for you? What's the memory of that time?

Fair lover

It's not fair

grief has insulated me in the fold of its arms

Fell in love with my wail

My tearful despair

It's not fair

that

It holds me like I'm its one and only

Yet beats me black and blue like

It wants me dead

Lemon Kiss

Grief is bitter
The lemons that life gives
To those who care
Those who try to catch their breath
While sipping stale air
Grief is sweet
Granulated pieces
Of how much we care
Grief is grounding
Pulling you down
Metallic
Grief, too
is bland
Broken monotony
A replay of a replay
Hurt that's numbing
And excruciating at the same time

Full

Grief is the emptiness
Of ripped wrapping paper
Used and useless
Still managing
To cover the entire floor

Write about where grief is not loud, but everywhere

Nowhere

grief is nothing but love bottled up
In cut-stained glass
Overflowing because it has nowhere to go
No heart to receive
No arms to hold
No home to mail holiday cards
Grief is the matter we made to exist
The moments
We force ourselves to never forget

A phone call

Screaming

All I heard was she's gone

It was then

my tears kissed concrete

Falling into the depths of my shadow

I had no yearning to claw myself out

My Screams converted to sound waves

A piercing current that drowned out the city a world away

From staring death in the eyes

gravity robbed me

Shattered me into a million pieces

I knew then

I would never be able

To put myself together again

Why me?

What did I do to taste the staleness

Of orphaned and ostracized

32 and motherless

33 and fatherless

My unborn children

left grandparentless

Why me?

Left lonely and lost

She taught me so much

Except how to live without her

How to find the road to recovery

There's no way I can begin

Why me?

Mad at God

Because out of all the billions of people

Why he had to rip my mama from me

My sun out the sky

Why me?

Envy

I cut eyes at women who still

Have access to the womb

Held in the mold of their mothers

The offspring still

Able to wrap themselves in their

Umbilical cords

Crossed in conversation

With their carriers

Bargaining

Capable of carrying courage

From their mother's chest

I Suck my teeth at

The idea of

Spoiled grandkids

Emergency contacts

Mother—daughter

Daddy's girl

And

The lie

That

A better day is coming

Write a poem that explains what makes you the angriest when thinking about your loved one not here physically

Bargaining

"If I could hold on a little longer, the light will bring me back home."

Grief

Is an ocean

Some days

W

    A

        V

            E

                S

Take us out

And leave us for dea

        (d)

& some days

It holds onto

(US)

for dear life

Ocean water can be calm, or it can roar like the mightiest lion. Write about how dichotomous grief is. How it has or can be both sides of a spectrum?

Trading

Holding a glass
I closed my eyes and prayed
For healing
For mercy
For God to let go
Give him back to a wretched world
Let him stunt in his Cadillac once more
Take my pictures
Burn them all
Just so he can click his camera once more
God give me my father back

Bag Lady

I keep your clothes in a suitcase

I pull out your sweater when I need you the most

I wrap your medium-sized sleeves halfway around my waist

Hoping they will hold just a portion of the hurt

Just for a little bit

I inhale deeply

The smell

Sweet and relentless

crying until wind is ripped me from

Crumbled and cremated

Eroded into pieces

Folded back into your sweater

Back packed in a suitcase

Until the next time

I plan to return back home

Silence

I didn't know grief would feel this quiet
The pause before the crash
Between whispers of the waves
Washing the sound of your vibrato away
Wondering if playing your voicemails will
Cover me in warm sand
Or cold broken rocks
Knowing too well
They're both the same

Uninvited Guest

Death knocks on doors with duality
An invitation to the beginning
Of grief and glory
Living and losing
Forgiving and forgetting
Salvation and separation
Holding both tomorrow's tears
And yesterday's memories
Asking to come in

Fireflies

Beginning Again

What's worse?

Falling or crashing

Gravity swept from under you

like family secrets

And Persian rugs

Like

Feenin' for finally

Cause the high is short

And the lows be too long

Or is it

The fear of the unknown

Brushing my hair gently past my ear

Whispering

Sweet nothings every time it's near

The piercing of the silence

Slits cut deeper

Than bloody wrists

Because at least

Knife in hand

The pattern I control it

Peace I can't find it

The stinch of rotting realization

That tomorrow is promised

To those who are still living

Broke and bottled

Only handled in portions

I'm scared I might lose

My potion

If I let grief suck me dry

I'm scared

To wither wilt and die

My deepest fear is

Forgetting how to cradle

My conscious

How to hold hope

And my head up

At the same time

I'm scared of quitting

But I'm more scared of beginning

Both

Some days I'm the mop

Cleaning corners of chaos

Other days I'm overflowing buckets of blame

Pieces of me found stained

In loose baseboards….

On the worst day

I'm both

Missed Call

I wish that loneliness didn't settle on my chest

The kind that's labored and lost for words

My phone would ring

Lines tangled with worry

Wrapped with "Are you ok?"

"Have you landed?"

"Did you make it home?"

I would be somebody's child again

I'd still send you straight to voicemail

Knowing I'd have tomorrow to call you back

And even then I'd rush you off the phone

For the friends you always told me I didn't have

I wish that I listened

Now I'm waiting patiently for your call

Searching my frontal cortex for your words

And warmth from this cold world

If you were granted one wish to rewrite a moment, a word, or a goodbye—what would you change, and why does that moment still live with you?

The middle of Goodbye

I lost my way
Yet I keep finding myself
Torn between
Walking away
Or finding a way to stay
I've come to terms with
The fact that
It hurts either way

Write about the moment when you realize you feel lost but are still searching for yourself

Depression

"Some nights the fireflies are nowhere

to be found"

Rambling

Depression is when the

relief from rawness

Is only found in deep sleep

So, seeking solitude seems better

Then facing fears

friends

Family who feel…

But can't understand

silently

Letting teardrop drain oceans

Filling my pillows with thoughts

Evaporating back

then

Transferring to my head

That I'll never be enough

Never be what I need

That I'll always push away

The wind beneath my wings

Put away my light

Because the pain

Keeps me perched in

The still of the night

Write a piece that starts with "depression is…"

Darkness

I've fallen into darkness

Cold and quiet

The walls won't speak

Even they're holding their breath

Damp and ghastly

Malignant and mourning

Chewed up and spit out

I've cried so hard

My chest sleeps in my abdomen

Pain pounds my temples

Kicking down dignity's door

Eyes piled high on flushed cheeks

Sinus suffocates my senses

I'm too weak to get up

Too afraid to look around

I'd rather sulk in solitude

Instead of finding my way out

At least here

You circulate my conscious

Massage my mind

And

Hover in my heart

At least here

My screams echo

Back as your name

Write from the perspective of the darkness itself. Why is it holding you? Is it protecting you or imprisoning you?

Unpacking Trauma

Our body keeps the score
our mind is committed to forgetting
times we didn't love it enough
to believe in its beauty
So, we filled our frame with lies
For all the times
We carelessly cuddled death
As if it would give us a better life
Come tomorrow

Settled in

January 11

January 31

April 5

April 11

April 22

May 23

June 13

July 21

August 1

October 6

November 11

December 30

While some say time heals

Some of us know

how it only tells

If infection has settled in

Swollen with fear

Pained to touch

No air to let it breathe

Just reminders

Of that moment

when grief first ripped us apart

And yet it still aches

Year after year

Visions of you

Sometimes I still see you

Sitting on the edge of your cigarette burned bed

The fumes from your Newport

Still linger in my hair

Til this day I scroll missed calls

Hoping to see your number there

I still replay old voicemails

Listen, cry, and laugh

Wishing I had more to hold on to

Than these messages from the past

Where do you still expect to see them? (chair, porch, voicemail, kitchen)

Season's greeting
From a broken heart
Hot chocolate and cold embraces
Empty stockings with your name
This Christmas
No wishing upon a tree's star
Would help me to see your light
Wrapped around my windowsill
Sits memories starting to fade
Visions of new normal
Reminds me that nothing
Will ever be the same
City colder
World lonelier
No Christmas carol could sing
Your song
Or your journey
loud enough

Unexpected Visitors

Today feels a little less heavy
But there are still unpacked boxes everywhere
I feel like grief leaves no room for the
Ones still living
For the beds we still must make
For those of us
Still breathing
It's suffocating here
Grief has found its way into
Every song and every picture
Positioned itself in between
Past memories and tomorrow's
"Damn, she still ain't gon call"
It has
Seeped out of closet spaces
And laid its clothes out
prepared them for tomorrow
Wearing out its welcome
This unexpected visitor
Without my permission
Has made my mind
Its new home

Tears for you

My eyes have somehow
Learned to bottle up everyone else's sadness
death and loss
To shed more tears for you
When someone dies
I cry out for you
I watch others grieve
And I grieve harder for you

Heavy

Just because I'm not hollering

Don't mean I ain't hurting

I've packed more pain in carry-ons

Layered more lies in luggage

Lost somewhere

Between

"I'm ok today"

And "Just manifest the negativity away"

Just because I carry it well

Don't mean it ain't heavy

Hoarding tears and trauma

My pain list requires commas

So when you see me

Know my smile

Is the only thing I can control

I weaponize it

Cut glass

Windows

Into a shattered soul

Alive

(To the rose bush in front of the house we were evicted from)

Tupac wrote about the rose
that grew from concrete
Like this one growing from hurt
Defying the odds
Blooming in the midst of death
Saturated deep in roots
Reminders of mornings
After a night of
overcoming
Withdrawing
Broke off by bay breezes
And cutthroat seasons
Yet withstanding
Death wishes and
Internal bleeding
Cause most time
We be the reason

Write a poem to something that survived when it shouldn't have—

a plant, a body, a version of yourself, a memory

Hidden

When I smile
Grief hides in the soles of my feet
Ten toes down in depression
Grounded in gray matter
Seeped into concrete
Warmth beneath cold streets
But they see the crease in my eyes
The arch of my grin
Little do they know I let grief win
I kissed death this morning
Wished it would take me too
Carry me to a place where I didn't
Have to simultaneously carry this smile
And harbor this
Death row of pain

Who Comforts the Water?

Nobody knows if water cries

the normalcy of its roar keeps us

satisfied

but who carries the burdens of

overflowing dams?

who helps rivers running away from

what torments it

Haven't you heard the Wailing of the

ocean

The Solemn Songs of the sea

big bodies of water like plus size girls

with low self-esteem

next to shallow and Shameless

the Pacific Ocean once confided in me

that she felt less beautiful

she said to me "I have comforted

thousands, but who comforts me?

feeling afraid because I don't know

where to even start or change

Where do I begin

I watch people over and over find

blessings in me...

fall in love but from a distance never

getting too deep

so how should I feel?

You find Me beautiful

but here I am drowning in my own

tears

Broken clocks

Depression feels like

Yesterday's forgotten memories

I can trace the feeling

Nevertheless

I can never put a finger on it

It feels like the first time

I realized I couldn't control the ocean

Even though I own saltwater stock

I can't even muster the strength

To drown in my own tears

It feels like I'm

Running

haphazardly

on fields

Gloves up

Trying to catch my...

... breath... and these hand

Blackened catfish

I don't even know who I am

Feels like knife kissing skin

Because I just want to feel again

Making love to what ifs

Stealing time with goodbyes

Because

The only thing I have enough of

Is the feeling of being out of time

Write about a moment when you felt disconnected from yourself. What did time feel like in that moment—slow, broken, rushing, or missing entirely? Describe the sensations, thoughts, and questions that lived in that space.

Acceptance

"And then one night, you find your
own light outside the jar"

Hopeful

I just hope my laughter is louder than my cries

This legacy is longer than the loss

That I continue riding

The waves

my ancestors

sent to cover me in courage

and

to enwrap me in resilience

Self-Love

(RIP bell hooks)

Today I give myself the love

I often dreamed of

Filled with forever

Laying artificial flowers at the end of my bed

Because while my growth is forever

I'm already fully bloomed

Could never be uprooted

bell said,

"Love is an action, not simply a feeling"

So, I pour into me

On the hardest day

and love my flawed features

unconditionally

Because that is

My most important job

Each & every day

Legacy Flows

There's a beauty in the uncontrolled
The Unleashed
Freedom wears fine as its primer
Flowing past barriers
Blocked paths
Finding its way to anywhere other
Then here
Moving past this moment
Of mere minute counting
Commutes to work
Tears for those we've lost
There's love in wilderness
In the leaves that died
And now live in the backdrop
Of a filtered memory
Flowing down this stream of life
There's reminders to never stop
Unsure of where you come from
Roots too deep to dig
History to rich to relive
This breeze is flowing
My grandmother speaking in tongues

Praying for my womb
For This world
Waiting to be uncovered
Sowed in the morning
Fed in the moonlight
Patience is growing
Thin
But God knows how to
Turn water to wine
So I know it'll flow
On her time
Sweetened with
This grind
No destination
It's the process
That legacy pursues
The journey
That shows the proof
Flowing
With no means to an end
Knowing at some point life will begin
Yet again
There's freedom here

Write about the release when you surrender to grief and experience freedom

Never Would Have Made It

Never would have made it
Your grace and mercy
Didn't make paths easier
But it ensured my
perseverance strengthened
Your prayers clothed me
Covered my tattoos in testimonies
Led me through tests
Blinded by faith
You never failed me
Blessed me with Blackness
Bold as the night
Filled with sight
And saving
So here I am
Eyes closed
Giving you every bit of praise
Because I know I'll have
A lifetime more
To write, dance, and sing
Your name...

Phoenix

In these moments of life when the
weight of your grief
Feels heavier than the remorse of your
survival
You question if you even have
The strength to grip the edge
Or gasp for air
Pulled back each time
By
The depths of care
The embrace of cold stares
Behind your own closed eyelids
Washed out tears
And weathered shores
Hard rocks break
Hard knocks shake
Quivering quietly
Hoping no one
Can see the crumbling
Of fate
The haunting of fears
Replaying memories
Because there's no more to make
I've learned
What isn't treasured
Is up for take
Squandered and slow
right
In front of your eyes
You learn to hold on to love tighter

Only for the wind
To snatch
The Flame from
Life's lighters
But
There is still a spark
A fire inside
That can only be extinguished
Through a specific form of death
—suicide
Tupac once said
"Death is not the greatest loss
The greatest loss is what dies while still
alive"
Because You can't kill those
Who never surrender
Who aren't afraid to allow grief to
enter
Wrap it tight
Like strangers
filled with lust in the heat of the night
In the flicker of light
my fingers tiptoe across her shadow
searching for ways finish her right
So I plot
And prey
Understanding
That I am in control
Of how long she stays

Cardinal

It's always in the midst of chaos
You visit with messages
Of motivation and memories
Filling me
With reminders you're still here
Now I pray
Little red bird
Come visit me today
Grandmothers Prayers
I am still being lifted
Whispered in the wind
Covered in grandmothers sugar
Strong like Folgers
Boiling hot
Watch the kettle
And the pot
Keep you eyes on your investment
We
Be cream of the crop
Prayers to never forget the bottom
But relive memories at the top
I hear her calling
Father, God
Guide my children to greatness
Take the drug taste from their mouth
Move addiction
From their body
Blanket my family
May your love never stop

In many cultures red cardinals Signals a deceased love one is trying to send me a message of comfort and reassurance. What signs have you received from your loved ones?

House Key

I still have your housekey around my keychain
I remember when you lit me up for losing it
Called me everything but a child of God
I had to knock everytime
Call to make sure you were nearby
I didn't find it until you were gone
Guess you wanted me to know
I'd always have a home

Scars

We are all as strong

as our deepest scars

But we must get past the hurt

That was endured

To find the beauty

Of the thickening of our skin

Good Friday

Granny died on Good Friday
It keeps me believing in Christianity's worth
bewildered at the thought of never hearing her voice
but when short beeps turned into one long tune
I knew that this wasn't permanent
that by Sunday
she would rise like
smoke from the menthols she used to smoke
like heat in buildings with no windows
like balloons not knowing their high will end
eventually
like Jesus
raised from the dead
Sunday school lessons of his resurrection
replayed in my head
Four years later
I still look forward to Easter Sunday
believing that she will show up to dinners I cook for her
shout, "Didn't I tell you to stop stirring in that gravy and glaze that ham again."
As the festivities begin
I light candles
igniting hope that will elevate to heaven's gates
praying she will see the light, smell the smoke, and know that
I am forever waiting for her to rise

I've come to terms with terror

The loneliness that haunts me

Like it knew what I did last summer

It watched me cower

Cry and crawl into darkness

I've come to terms with tears

Random and wild

Roaring rivers

I've come to terms with drowning

I no longer try to swim

Resilience

Down at dusk

Darkness always comes

Doubt and despair

Positioned between

Crescent moons and care

Coping with loss of self

Only loneliness left burning there

Lingering between clouds

And skylines

But each day

She manifests strength

Streams of her fiery tears

Creep past

The ones who doubted her last

And she rises

Like tides

Strong

And Strategizing

A way to

Blanket other lost souls

Remember me

Remember me for my ambition
For the time I swallowed the wind
Regurgitated whispers
Both wild and roaring
Wrapped in aspirations affixed
In between now and near
Beyond insecurity and fear
Remember me for my smile
For the time I swallowed the moon
Orbited planets and people
Wrapped in rainbows
Black magic
And
Golden undertones
Remember me as the under dog
For the time I swallowed the opponent
Digested disbelief and doubt
And fought my way out

With you

With you
closet doors are cracked
never been compelled to hide my brokenness
I invited you into my darkness
Daring you to embrace what is isn't illuminated
In between my laughter and light
You found beauty in blackness
The dirt that surrounds my cold corpse
Because I've been dead before
But you celebrated my birth each time
Planted flowers around my tombstone
To show I am still growing … So
My skeletons dance for you
Expose the scars beyond their bones
Brittle… breaking under pressure
But you collected the ash and made me over
Took your hands and held me in hurt
Held a mirror to my face
Not to show my flaws but to
Show me there would never be a reason to hide
That you fit perfectly in my frame
That you could caress me
While I dangled over the edge of regret
That you would love me
Through sunrise
And keep me warm after sunset

Grief is

Grief is the emptiness

Enveloped

Between the love letters & hate mail to God

Praising for taking her suffering away

While blaming for taking my mama away

Grief is a bottomless well

Because who knew I could cry

This well or this long?

Clawing my way out

But grief is strong

It manipulates

And waits

When you think you got a grip

It's latches back on

Grief is the kiss between

Dust and wind

Sweeping reality

That our memory making

Has come to an end

& a new chapter begins

Grief is a book with no cover to judge

No spine to hold

Just blank tear stained pages

Out of order

Tatted and overrun

And for some reason

I keep reading

Hoping one day

I can comprehend some

Write a poem that defines grief multiple times—and lets every definition contradict the last

Start Over

My Fireflies:

"The light that never left"

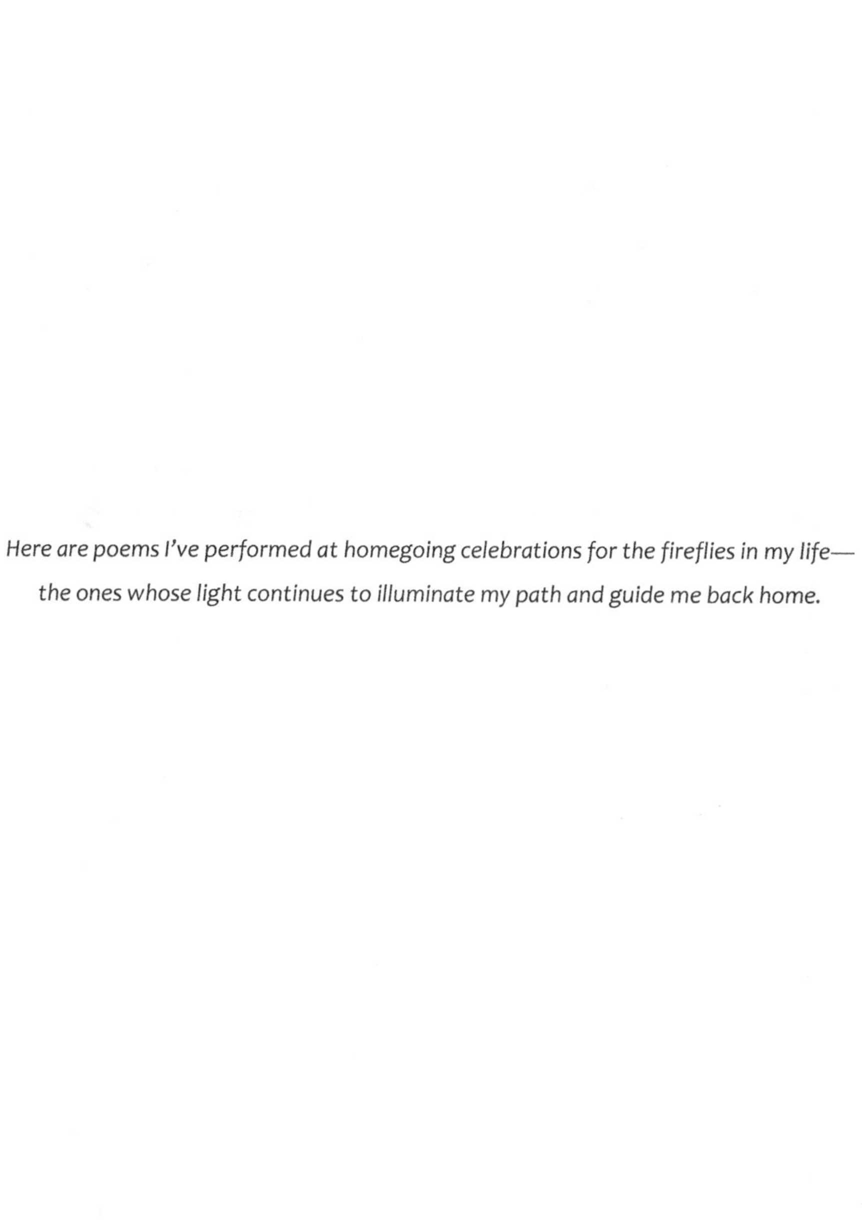

Here are poems I've performed at homegoing celebrations for the fireflies in my life—
the ones whose light continues to illuminate my path and guide me back home.

Aishiteru

Teruko K. Dobashi

1/11/1921-06/13/2017

Obachan,
Between Golden Gate Bridges and fog
nestled beaches
The avenues will never be the same
I remember
Dim sum from Balboa and Japanese
cinema
Walks from Presidio and
that day in 7th-grade when I found out
I was allergic to pineapples
I missed 1st through 7th period
I laid in your bed
You checked on me often
I remember
Ginger snaps, green tea, and snap peas
Days when sun seeped in window
And we found home in bar stools and
kitchen counters
Often you sang hymns of Japanese
countrysides
Or serenaded the waves of your love
washing over ojichan and the rest of us
Praising my father and aunties alike
for their undeniable commitment
You taught me how to be grateful for
the unyielding love of family
I remember

You teaching me how to write my
name.. Your name… our name in
hiragana
Often mispronounced misspelled and
misunderstood
Yet I stand diligently defined as "bright
child" "Illuminate child" "Sunshine
child"
I bask in that glory
Regardless of what city or state I reside
I know that you're the best light of me
shining inside
You elucidate my ability to transcend
and inspire
Although, there are princesses,
scientists, & emperors who share our
name
none of them equate to you
For you are cultivated from crescents
of moonlit smiles
Serenity, style, & grace
Guiding our family
You empower me
equipped me with drive,
determination, & passion
To always remind myself to prevent
trials from turning into tribulations
& injustices from becoming my reality
Obachan,

Although I never fully learned how to

speak, write, & translate Nihongo

I find solace in trying

I remember Ogichan would ask me

Wakimashita?

Do you understand?

And my answer would be wakirimasen

I don't

But I remember

you showing me characters in the Nichi

Bei Times

And the excitement in my voice

the first time I could sing

the entire first verse of Sukiyaki to you

While I'm still learning linguistically

I've compiled characteristics of your

truths

that have shaped me into the womyn I

am today

Shojikina Tokoro- Your honesty

Your ability to be brave and bold

From your embraces that blanketed

my beautiful Brown skin while

simultaneously scolding me for

another

tattoo

or putting on too much weight

One minute later

Smiling

asking me if I'm hungry

Have I eaten?

I felt your love and I knew you cared

Kandaina-

Your generosity poured into us all

You have generated generations of

caretakers, educators, risk-takers

Beautifully brilliant and never broken

A giver

Only ever receiving your grandkids and

great grandkids with open arms,

laughter, and love

Tsuyoi to ushikushi

Your strength and beauty

Bestowed upon me

A Dobashi womyn

Strong minded

molded from

Jasmine, matcha, &

Almond shaped eyes

Kaishikoi

Your intelligence

Perseverance and pride in the work

you've accomplished

The accolades you gained

Gave me gateways to keep going

Keep giving

Keep striving

Obachan,

I realize I am

because you were

Honest, generous, strong, beautiful,

and intelligent

I can never thank you enough

For molding me

believing in me when I didn't believe in

myself

Loving me across state lines

Encouraging me to continue to change

lives

Today I vow to ensure your legacy

lingers

In our hearts forever

That your smile and memories will

always light up rooms

That I will always remember my worth

My strength

My ability to succeed

With you watching over me

Obachan

Aishiteru

I love you

The Light

Avis Hughley

4/11/1964-1/31/2025

There are so many questions I wish I
had answers to…
Like how even in the darkest hour
Your smile still shined bright
Your Heart and mind stayed
Filled with all that was right
Compassion and care
Creviced in your character
Cuddled in each curl
How did you learn to draw
Color in cursive
Create In calligraphy
More importantly
How were you able make everyone feel
As if they belonged
Loving and accepting us for exactly
who we are
Your encouragement and love
Carried me this far
First week at Toomer
I was Trembling with fear faced with
insecurity
but it was You who pulled me aside
Whispered to me to remember I was
good enough
you said Pray and believe… because
God is always near
How did you never miss a moment to
honor someone

Support a dear friend
You showered those around you with
tokens
Of appreciation
My favorite is the Maya Angelo coin
The thoughtfulness in your words
Every handwritten card
My first week as a principal in my own
school
You walked into my office
With wise words and a crystal bowl in
hand
Reminding me to always trust in God's
plan
I still want to know
How were you wired with
righteousness
Wrapped in worthy
To give so generously
To spread love so wide
Gifts cards and wisdom
Smiles and unyielding care
I wish I knew
how you wore patience like armor
Serenity like soft pearls
Calmness in chaos
You- were walking warmth in this cold
world

Every child at Toomer wanted an

embrace

Every adult yearned for one as well

You, Mrs Hughley, are the image I see

when they say

God's love never fails

He spoke blessings through you

Similar to him you healed souls too

I still want to know

How were you able to spread kindness

like wildfires

Joy like breadcrumbs

To so many of us lost —- you felt like

home

When I lost my mom you were there

Holding me tight— praying for me day

& night

Telling me trust God

He will carry me through

15 months later When my dad passed

You reminded me

Through scriptures and prayers

That God would never leave me

And I would always be loved by you

An earth angel I can say that I knew

You … have been a lot of our north

stars

The optimism that the world might

not be so wretched

So filled with wrong

Because you are the tune made from

God's best song

Your smile illuminated the Lord's best

work

He used his best brushes on you

Colored inside each line

perfected his canvas on you

Dear God

I don't want to question your decisions

But why take away world peace

Our sliver of hope and positivity

But I guess heaven was in chaos

and you needed her calm spirit

To awaken the light to guide lost souls

In the dark of the night

To Big Rob, i hear her saying do right

To lil Robert-I pray her memories will

blanket you

Share warm reminders that she's all

around

Because any good deed

Is a reminder to her seed

That greatness grows inside of you too

Her greatest legacy is you

Your mom— carried your

achievements

Close to her heart

you were the light of her life

When the sea of grief is loud and

roaring

Remember one of her favorite quotes

Philippians 4:13

I can do all things in Christ who

strengthens me

Fireflies

You will feel her even though you may

not see

I hope you find comfort in the fact that

your mom

Touched so many lives

She healed so many souls

Ms. Hughley

your Cook, Whitefoord and Toomer

family

Was blessed with your presence

28 years of molding bright minds

Pride fills 65 Rogers' st Bricks

You are the cement that keeps us

together

We will remember you forever

And when we need an example of

excellence

We will lift your name

and from now on

Being granted God's greatest gift

Will be all of our claim to fame

I love you forever

Greedy

Phillip Hamilton

4/5/1960-5/23/2025

Dear God

guide me through this hurt

Navigate me nearest to numbness

Because recently

there's been no rest for the weary

No pause for the strong

I just want a moment to catch my

breath

Believe that you've shared this level of

pain with the rest

But honestly, I know that

Grief is no stranger to us all

We're here

Because yet another real one had to

fall

And

Rise to your kingdom

Removed from these worldly woes

I just ask you God to

not let this agony

Show

Situate its bags under my restless eyes

Grant more gray hair to freely fly

Display broken hearts

In the palm of my hands

Find suffering stuffed into despair

Dear God tell

Greedy I'll miss his laugh

Echoing in the pit of my sternum

Situating itself in the memory bank

Depositing love that only you could

create

Forged our bond through blood

An uncle but more like father

I hope he's watching over me from

above

I sift through those church days

When Granny was gone

We would raid the cabinets

Create a meal made with

whatever we could find

We had nothing but time

Watch movies all day

You'd talk through it all

Like you had seen it before

you would tell the ending

I'd believe you

So, you'd be dead wrong

We'd laugh and laugh

Until granny got home

Dear God tell him

He's the reason I'm this big

As a kid I remember rushing to get my

plate

I knew I had to before greedy did

He's the reason I'm this brave

Walk in rooms like God sent me there

He's the reason I'm this fly

Posing to be chosen

Because you couldn't tell him he

wasn't that guy

Dear God, I ask you to send me signs

That your blessings may not be when I

want

But they always on time

I ask you to cover me in memories

That mask this jaded face

To send me joy to stand in losses place

I ask you to carry me past affliction

Turn me around

And

Place me on solid ground

God

Shield me from the truth that

I won't see His face no more

Won't come home to tell him about

Atlanta

And my crazy life so far

Won't be able to take him to eat

To hug him in the middle of Mission

and 6th street

Won't be able to cry to him about my

mama

his sister no more

Look to him for strength

dear God

Tell him thank you for loving me

Like his own daughter

For protecting me

Thank him for reminding

That as he walks through that golden

gate

That now the warrior lies in me

To my Father

Michael K. Dobashi

6/13/1953-10/6/2024

To my father

Who taught me many lessons

Who instilled in me many words

Even still when your voice only

lingers in the rustling of the trees

The pause between songs

The roar of the ocean

The solemness in the sea

I'm reminded of you

Every morning

Through this unyielding desire to

Continue our

Regashii

this legacy

Lifted in my lungs

Light gleaming from your

Temple

Wisdom wedged between

Your core

see You

Guided me down roads

Winding with possibilities

you reminded me

With courage I could have anything in

this world

Your lil girl with big ambitions

Wouldn't be half of the woman I am

today

Without your interventions

Your prayers

long talks and well wishes

You Blanketed me with the belief

That Dobashi

Not only means a bridge made of earth

But that we are grounded with

greatness

Rooted with resilience

Wrapped with Warrior

Packaged with perseverance

This pride seeps from our soul

radiating Red suns and Black fists

You have embodied genes of a pioneer

Preparing the world for sweet scents

Of melting pots

America's best Blessings

3 children and 7 grandchildren later

Creating empires of embellished bi and

tri-racialness

We are cut from a different cloth

Beautifying San Francisco

Creating a love unparallel

To my father

Who taught me how to

Aishiteru

Love

Stringing me along melodies of some

of the best songs

Subsequently

Bestowing

Upon me my

Love for lyrics

My love for words

Thumbing base guitars

Gap bands

Temptations

34 years later

Until forever

I'll always be

Your lil girl

You taught me frugality

Bargaining

Hustling

How to catch a deal

But you were never stingy with your

love

To my father

Who taught me about

Hokori ni omou

Pride

Pressed against my chest

Chiseled in my soul

Holding my head high

4 college degrees later

Everything I accomplish

I do it for you

Rising up 8 times after all 7 falls

I know strength is written on all our

walls

etched into our eternity

Everlasting

Your legacy will live on

To my Father

Who taught me about Kazoku

family

Because we all we got

Eric Darryl and I will carry your load

Lift your name in lights

Make sure your story is told

The magnificent 7

Will make rumbles from heaven

Unfold

Success impressed

In their hearts and

Your name will be sang in their homes

Your wife

Will hold your heartbeat

And ensure

In the face of adversity

Our family won't succumb to defeat

To my father

Who taught me shashin

To capture each moment

Marvel in

The world around me

Noticing the beauty in every frame

Snap after snap

Who knew a 5x7

Could capture love over so many

decades

Developing each image

Live and living color

A memory is priceless
But each picture
Worth gold
Friends and family
I ask you to
All Pause to reflect
Each photo he took of you
And the story it told
Remember his face
His smile
His kindness
The light his legacy still holds
To my father
Who taught me my first Japanese song
My next karaoke gone wrong
Sounds a lil like this
Oemuite Arukō namida ga ko borei nai
yoni
Omeida su haru no hi hi Tori bo chi no
yoru
I look up as I walk
So that tears won't fall
Remembering those spring days
And today I'm all alone
I'm trying to stay strong

To my father
I hold on to a
Japanese proverb
professing the love of life
Tonbi Ga Taka Na Uma
A kite breeding hawks
Thank you for steering us
The best way you knew how
Blowing us in the breeze
Teaching us just how to be
Wild passionate and free
Truly believing we couldn't
Have a better father
I pay homage to you
I love you always
Dear daddy
Your legacy lives on
we will always celebrate your life
Don't worry don't fret
Ease your soul
Take your rest
Because today tomorrow
And forever
You will be Bay Area's Best

She Felt like Church

Ruby Mae Hamilton

08/01/1921-04/22/2011

Ruby couldn't drive but she was driven

God fearing

Found routes to Spiritual kitchens

Seasoned salvation

Care filled cooking

pot filled smiles filled to brim

She Poured love in her food

pain in her prayers

She was the closest I've ever been to Righteousness riddled in flesh

A Christian womyn

But ain't too holy to tell you how it is

Or how it could be if you tried to get a plate

Past 10-

shit anytime after it made its way to be packed

She embodied versatility

She clutched pearls and pistols

Cooked rice without measure

My granny was from the hood

I bet she could eyeball purp

She-herself- felt like church

Like hope in human form

Like her Sunday singing

Was straight from psalms

In these crops-she was the cream

From Louisiana to Cali

All fueled by a dream

I cry—Cause now I can only see her in mine

Dear Mama

Regina Lynn Hamilton

12/30/1962-07/21/2023

Dear mama,

Where do I start...

All these rambling thoughts in my

mind

Thinking of you is how I've passed my

time

My world has been upside down

Since you've been gone

Gravity has given up on me

& 15 days later I'm still falling

Catching myself still calling your phone

Still longing for more

yearning for home in the corners of

your arms

each time I wake up

I feel like I'm being robbed once more

My sun snatched from my sky

You always said you love me to the

moon

And back

But how long is this trip?

Life has been passing me by

As I wait for you to rotate

in more than just my mind

Because selfishly

I want this all to be a lie

Dear mama,

I know you don't want me saying the

word lie

But maybe if I say it enough you will

come back

To slap this bitter taste out my mouth

Loneliness sits underneath my tongue

Like that man on the dock of the bay

I think he left his heart in San Francisco

Like God took his mama away

They say when life gives you lemons

Make lemonade

But they didn't tell you how bad it

stings

Dear mama,

I been waiting on my phone to ring

Since you been gone I aint had no

sugar

So I feel like I don't have all the

ingredients

To make it

You're missing

& my Heart is wrecked at sea

Searching for you

A get away

From These salty tears

Because

The what ifs

I should haves

Been drowning me

See what do I without my mama

This world is cold

I can't breathe
Can't believe you're gone
I'm all alone
Dear mama
I still have so many questions
Like how many times have you been in love?
What are you most proud of?
Who was your first kiss?
And what was your last wish?
Did you trade in being my mama
To get back to yours?
Knock on God's door
And ask to come home?
To leave this world of worry
Home of hurt
Dear mama
I know I sound mad, but
I'm still so proud of you
For breaking free
For living your last years responsibly
Doing yo thug thizzle while
Whipping a Honda 2023
Was doing better
Than a lot
Liberating your light
Out of life's glass jar
But you left me here
To wallow in this darkness
Dear mama,
Thank you
For being my vessel
For carrying me in your best smile

For
molding me
hard outer shell
Resilience found floating around
placenta
Hustla's ambition wrapped around
umbilical cord
Cultivated in corners of creativity and crazy
I miss the way you cuss in poetry
Pray in plays
Pave ways from no ways
Dear mama,
Thank you
For nurturing me
9th grade drop out
But trauma survivors be the best teacher
You never failed me
Blessed me with Blackness
Bold as the night
Filled with sight
You told me to always be aware of my surroundings
Set it off if they trying me
Dear mama
I heard the Apple doesn't fall far from the tree
And here I be...
Your seed
Sowed in city soil
Saturated with love
Lingering in your Light

You nourished me

Taught me how to embrace wrong

And embody right

So

Sneak me the number to heaven

I'd collect calls all night

Play on Jesus's phone

Just to

So here I am

Eyes closed

Giving you every bit of praise

Because I know I'll have

A lifetime more

To write, dance, and sing

Your name

Mama

Your laugh is on God's favorite playlist

Dear mama,

You're the one who taught me

That some hits take the wind out of

you

Dear mama

I ain't gon lie

I can still feel your protection

Lingering in the wind

11/11

Guardian Angel

Save me a spot beside you and granny

in heaven